MINI MAKING FOR BEGINNERS

The Picture Step By Step Instructional Guide on How to Create and Make Miniature Polymer Clay Food from Scratch at Home

Boris Joseph

Copyright@2021

TABLE OF CONTENT

CHAPTER 1 3

INTRODUCTION...3

CHAPTER 2 5

TOOLS FOR POLYMER CLAY MINI FOOD 5

CHAPTER 3 16

HOW TO MAKE MINI FOOD FROM CLAY 16

THE END 41

CHAPTER 1

INTRODUCTION

There are so many various sorts of Polymer Clay artists/hobbyists out there, and each of us uses a distinct set of tools and equipment that we find to be most effective for our own needs.

My work is largely concerned with the creation of tiny foods, and the following are some of the instruments that I employ. Polymer Clay is a wonderful material, and the equipment we use to work with clay can help us improve our skill.

The tools that I am going to share here are only a few of the most important ones that I use on a daily basis. I also work with various mediums like as resin, air dry clay, and other materials. However, I will just show you the ones that I use in conjunction with the polymer clay in this tutorial. My tool collection has increased substantially in the last four years, so if you are a newbie in the art of tiny food creation, keep in mind that you will not need everything. The nicest part about producing tiny meals is that you can already create a wide variety of dishes with only the most basic of equipment and ingredients.

CHAPTER 2

TOOLS FOR POLYMER CLAY MINI FOOD

Instruments of a fundamental nature

If you are interested in creating miniatures out of polymer clay, you will not want a large quantity of clay, but having a range of colors will be beneficial. Instead of purchasing entire bars of color, get a pack of sample colors, which will provide you with a vast array of colors to choose from. It's also worth mentioning that tiny food producers primarily use white and transparent clay, so I tend to buy large bars of them as well as Sculpey Ultralight when I'm shopping (not in photo).

Translucent Liquid Sculpey (Liquid clay) is also necessary in tiny food creation since it will be used to create a variety of different products in the end. During the month of June, I will be creating a tutorial particularly for this topic.

WHERE TO GET LIQUID SCULPEY

You may use transparent Liquid Sculpey to glue bits of polymer clay together, but I like to use Sculpey's Oven Bake Clay Adhesive especially because it is tackier than Liquid Sculpey and hence easier to work with than the former. When cured, Bake and Bond becomes hard (much like polymer clay and TLS), therefore I find myself using it a lot when I need to join two pieces of jewelry together.

Miniature makers tend to use relatively little clay while creating miniatures, thus it is quite common for them to keep a large supply of old clay on hand. With Sculpey Clay Softener, on the other hand, you can make nearly any old clay look like new again!

If you wish to roll out consistent sheets of clay, a clay conditioning machine is required. Making do with a rolling pin alone is not an easy task! In addition, it may be used to create Skinner mixes, which will offer your tiny models a deeper color palette.

MACHINE FOR CONDITIONING CLAY IN THE SHOP

Blades and an X-acto knife are frequently employed in any endeavor, while a needle is employed to texture and shape clay

Texturing tools such as an old toothbrush and a recycled (but clean) aluminum foil are the most versatile. Keep an eye out for anything that has the ability to create texture since you can preserve it.

mold-making instruments

Especially if you are not creating figures, modeling tools may be quite beneficial, even if you only start with the most basic plastic ones available. Ball tools are also a good investment because they are often used and are available in a variety of sizes.

Molds and cutters are extremely important to any miniaturist who works with small scale models. It saves you time and ensures that you always receive a precise size and cut. Keep an eye out for cutters used in sugarcraft as well as any other tiny items you can discover! As long as it is appropriate for the scale, it may be used to create a variety of various objects. I also have a large number of Premo cutter sets that are not listed here.

Paints and colors are used in this process.

Use of alcohol inks on dried clay produces results that are virtually instantaneous in their drying time. It is also possible to paint on clay with acrylic colors, and to tint TLS with oil paint. Acrylic colors may be found here.

Pastels are used to create the shade on your miniature, which gives it a more realistic appearance. For added color, you may shave some into the TLS mixture as well. It is very difficult to go through a full piece of pastel, so make sure you purchase a box that is half the normal size.

materials used in the molding process

Molds save you time by allowing you to duplicate anything in a short amount of time. I make use of a Japanese mold that may be used again and again. After it has been softened in hot water and hardened again within minutes, it may be used immediately. A silicone mold is equally helpful and simple to use; simply combine one part of silicone with one part of water and you're ready to go! Given that I don't use much for miniatures, I typically just acquire a little quantity at a time, since they don't survive very long in my collection. It is also an excellent tool for sculpting and sanding once the epoxy Putty has been fully dried. It's what I use most often to create the forms for the molds. As with the silicon mold, I only receive a tiny box at a time because you will need to use it up fast as well.

Putting the finishing touches on it

For the final touches, I rely on a variety of Tamiya Decoration Series tools (this is only a fraction of the collection I have!).

Glazes assist to lock in the colors of your miniature and also provide a level of realism to it. I have matte and gloss varnishes that are water-based and can be used on polymer clay, as well as other materials.

The Dessert Topping Master is essentially colored PVA glue that when cured by air will provide the appearance of genuine sauces on top of desserts. Puffy

Paint, any sort of 'deco' gel, and sauces are some of the additional options available. This will also give your miniatures a greater sense of realism and depth.

Brushes are not only important for painters, but they are also useful for polymer clay artists. It is generally employed for the purpose of darkening clay. You may even use make-up brushes to paint on the finishing glaze/varnish after the clay has been allowed to set.

When working with polymer clay, wet wipes are needed to clean the equipment and to keep your hands as clean as possible. Because it is manufactured from the same composition as clay, PVA glue may be used to join pieces of clay (cured or uncured) together. You may also use PVA glue as a lacquer to give your project a semi-gloss appearance. When working with really sticky clay, talcum powder comes in handy, as does dusting molds prior to utilizing them.

Purchase little tiles rather than large ones in order to be able to work on many projects at the same time.

CHAPTER 3

HOW TO MAKE MINI
FOOD FROM CLAY

With the exception of the
baking, they are simple tasks
that take little time to complete

Supplies

The Clay consists of the following elements:

• Dark brown in color

• Light brown in color

Tan is a color that may be found in nature (lighter than the light brown)

- The color white

- The color black

- The color gray

- The color red

- The color orange

- Light Orange in color
- The color yellow

- The color green

- The color blue

- The color purple

- The color pink

The first step is to prepare the hamburger.

a: Remove the a:

For the bottom bun, use a light brown circular.

The onion ring is represented by a white circle.

The tomato is represented as a red circle.

The beef patty is represented by a dark brown circle.

The cheese is represented by a yellow circle.

The top bun is a light brown circular with a light brown border.

Finally, decorate the top with a few little white dots to represent sesame seeds.

Step 2: Making the Taco

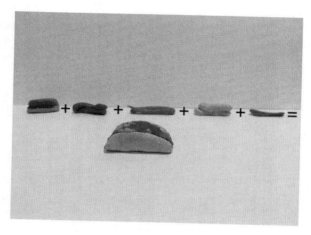

Make a taco shell out of tan clay by cutting a circle out of it. It should be folded in half like a taco shell. Fill the bottom of the shell with dark brown clay to serve as a base for the meat. Then, for the lettuce, sprinkle some green clay on top of everything. On finish the taco, add some orange clay to the top to serve as cheese. Finally, a small amount of red clay for the spicy sauce should be added.

The Third Step: The Sandwich

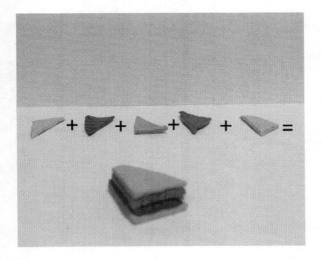

Cut out two triangles of the tan clay to use as bread pans for the bread. Cut a triangle of brown clay for the meat, an orange clay for the cheese, and a triangle of green clay for the

lettuce to finish the dish. Tada!
It's a sandwich!

The Fourth Step: The Pizza

For the pizza crust, you will cut
a circle of light brown clay to the
desired size. For the cheese, cut
off a circle of yellow clay using a
sharp knife. Toss on a few
extras.

The Hotdog is the fifth step.

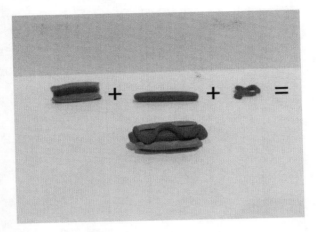

For the hot dog bun, cut a
rectangle out of the tan clay
using a sharp knife. Combine a
small amount of the red clay
with a small amount of the
brown clay to achieve a nice hot
dog hue. Form a cylinder out of
the reddish-brown clay that you
just prepared for the hot dog
with your hands. Finish it off
with a little strip of red or yellow

clay for ketchup or mustard, depending on your preference.

In the sixth step, there is the fried egg.

Begin by forming a little frying pan out of aluminum foil, and then placing an egg white and yolk in the bottom.

The Seventh Step: The Donut

Make a little donut form out of the tan clay and set aside. As a finishing touch, place a circle of pink clay (or any other color) on top of the cake as icing.

Step 8: The Spaghetti Cooking Process

To begin, place the plate on the table. Make a circle of white clay for the plate by cutting it out with a knife. There is no need to include further information unless you want to. Then add the pasta to the pan. To make the spaghetti, roll up a piece of tan clay until it is thin and uniform, then put it onto a serving dish. In a final step, stir in the spaghetti sauce and a few meatballs. You may even include a little fork if you so choose!

the loaf of bread in the ninth step

The bread is straightforward; simply form a basic loaf shape and then draw some lines on top of it.

Step ten: Carving the Pumpkin

To begin, flatten the orange clay into a cylindrical form and set it aside. Then, using the brown clay, create a stem for the piece. Finally, draw a few lines around the pumpkin, starting at the stem and finishing at the base of it.

The Bananas are the eleventh step.

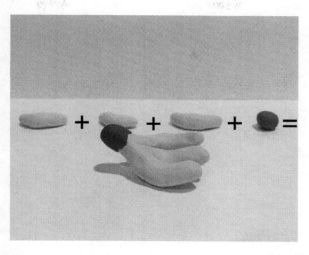

Make three banana shapes out of the yellow clay to begin with, then set them aside. Then place them next to one other and squeeze the tips of their heads together until they form a bunch of bananas. Finally, attach a little piece of brown clay to the top of the vase to serve as the stem.

Step 12: Preparing the Pretzel

Roll out a piece of tan clay until it is thin and uniform in thickness. After that, roll it into a pretzel form.

The Creamsicle (Step Thirteen)

Make a popsicle form out of
orange clay and set it aside. To
make a bite mark, cut a semi-
circle out of one of the top
corners of the paper. In the
interior of the bite mark, apply a
little amount of white clay.
Finally, insert a popsicle stick
into the bottom of the container.

The Orange and the Apple (Step 14)

Begin by forming two balls of clay, one of orange clay (for the orange) and one of red clay (for the red) (for the apple). Add some stems and leaves to both of them.

Step 15: The Gratification

The yellow clay should be used to form a wedge. Fill up the

blanks with details such as holes or biting marks.

The Mushroom (Second Step)

With the brown clay, form a half-circle with your hands. Make a sturdy stem out of the white clay and insert it into the vase.

The Potato (Second Step)

Make a loaf of bread-like form out of the dough. Make little adjustments to achieve a nice potato form. Make a few little markings and pockets.

Step 18: Beet and Cucumber Preparation

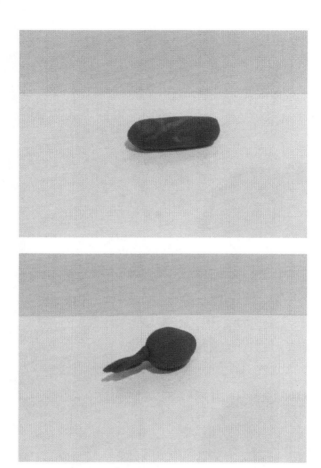

To make the beet, roll out a ball
of red clay and attach a short,
dark green stem to the center.

To make the cucumber, roll out a cylinder of dark green clay and add a small amount of lighter green clay to the bottom of the cylinder.

The Eggplant is the 19th step.

For the eggplant, make a cylinder out of dark purple clay and roll it out. To finish it off, add a dark green, leafy stem to the top.

The Pea Pod is the twenty step.

For the peas, roll out three balls of green clay on a work surface. For the pea pod, roll out a strip of green clay the width of the pod. In order for the peas to have a slight peeking out appearance, fold the pea pod around them and tuck the ends in.

THE END

Made in the USA
Columbia, SC
10 January 2024